THERE IS NO DIFFERENCE BETWEEN TIME AND ANY
OF THE THREE DIMENSIONS OF SPACE. . . .
WHAT GOES UP MUST COME DOWN. . . . ANY TWO BODIES IN
THE UNIVERSE ATTRACT EACH OTHER WITH A FORCE
THAT IS DIRECTLY PROPORTIONAL TO THE PRODUCT OF
THEIR MASSES. . . . THE EARLIEST CHINESE MAGNETIC
COMPASSES WERE PROBABLY NOT DESIGNED FOR
NAVIGATION BUT RATHER TO ORDER AND HARMONIZE THEIR
ENVIRONMENTS. . . . THE WHOLE IS GREATER THAN THE
SUM OF ITS PARTS. . . . FOR EVERY ACTION, THERE IS AN
EQUAL AND OPPOSITE REACTION. . . . TROPISM: THE
TURNING OF ALL OR PART OF AN ORGANISM IN A
PARTICULAR DIRECTION IN RESPONSE TO AN EXTERNAL
STIMULUS. . . . ALL CHARGED OBJECTS ARE ATTRACTED TO
OPPOSITE ELECTRIC CHARGES. . . . NEWTON DECLARED
THAT COLORS OPPOSITE EACH OTHER HAD THE
STRONGEST CONTRAST AND HARMONY. . . .

BEEKMAN 1802

Style

BEEKMAN 1802

Style

THE ATTRACTION OF OPPOSITES

BRENT RIDGE AND JOSH KILMER-PURCELL

A **CountryLiving** BOOK

RODALE

Rodale books may be purchased for business or promotional use or for special sales. For information, please write to:

Special Markets Department, Rodale Inc., 733 Third Avenue, New York, NY 10017

Country Living is a registered trademark of Hearst Communications, Inc.

Printed in China

Rodale Inc. makes every effort to use acid-free ♾, recycled paper ♻.

Book design by Galen Smith / Hardscrabble Projects

Library of Congress Cataloging-in-Publication Data is on file with the publisher.

ISBN 978–1–62336–507–3

Distributed to the trade by Macmillan

2   4   6   8   10   9   7   5   3   1   hardcover

We inspire and enable people to improve their lives and the world around them.
rodalebooks.com

For Uncle Arthur, who always used to boast that his house had been featured in *Architectural Digest*. Dear Arthur, we have an entire book now!

Thanks for the inspiration,
Brent and Josh

Contents

Introduction

chem·is·try \ˈke-mə-strē\ *noun*
1. the investigation of the ways in which substances interact, combine, reorganize, and change; and the use of these processes to form new substances

PEOPLE COME INTO RELATIONSHIPS with all sorts of emotional baggage, and they come with plenty of bags, boxes, box trucks, and storage units full of physical stuff, too. But these things don't have to weigh you down. With a little ingenuity, a thoughtful eye, some teamwork, and sometimes a little elbow grease, you can make a home together of all the things that you both treasure. Whether you are sharing a space with a best friend or a romantic partner, the space should (and easily can) reflect the tastes of everyone calling it home.

When we met in 1999, we could not have been more different.

Josh had been living a double life in New York City for several years: junior advertising executive by day and nightlife impresario by night (in other words, a drag queen named Aquadisiac).

Brent was a fresh-to-the-city young doctor from the South still wearing the Bible belt cinched tightly around his waist.

What they say is true. You can't help whom you fall in love with, and opposites really do attract. But at Beekman 1802, we like to think of it as two things coming together to make something complete.

We dated for 2 years before moving in together into a small studio apartment in the city's West Village.

The first home we purchased was a one-bedroom apartment in Manhattan's Upper East Side (pictured below). Like most new home owners, we had very little budget for decorating or remodeling, so we bought a few cans of paint and did our best to add a little drama to what was essentially a white box. After a flood and a necessary gut renovation, that apartment went on to be featured on *Apartment Therapy* and *The Martha Stewart Show* and in the *New York Post* and *Martha Stewart Living* magazine.

In 2008, we lost our jobs amidst the Great Recession, and we moved to a 200-year-old farm in upstate New York.

As we crossed the threshold for the first time, we looked at what greeted us not as a large, empty space but as a well for inspiration. Taking a little bit of this and a little bit of that, a little from our past lives in the city, and some new rural finds, the house became our home.

Those rooms and the surrounding 60 acres gave birth to our famed lifestyle brand, Beekman 1802—where city meets country in an unexpected and incredible way in every single item the company designs.

Now the historic Beekman Farm (built in 1802), and its unique style, has been featured in *Country Living, Vanity Fair, Food & Wine, Out, House Beautiful, Elle Décor, FOLK, Vogue,* the *New York Times, Sweet Paul, Design*Sponge, iVillage,* and *Anthology.*

Very few of us will ever have the luxury of having a complete house makeover. We don't move into an empty space and start completely new. We live in blended environments that evolve over time. We inherit, salvage, and purchase items as life rolls on. Things come and go—but our personality and style always remain.

In a recent study, 85.7 percent of participants claim to want a life partner who has their opposite traits. And why not? If you think about it, all the world is based on the attraction of opposites (positives and negatives, cations and anions, protons and electrons). Why should the physical world that we create around us be any different? The attraction of opposites can result in a more complete and visually interesting room.

In addition to showing studies from our own home, for this book we combed through the archives of *Country Living* magazine—documenting homes of everyday people for more than 20 years—to find inspiration and examples that will demonstrate how to create beautiful, practical rooms even when the items you have to work with might not immediately look like they belong together . . . just like us.

—Brent and Josh

CHAPTER ONE

OLD MEETS NEW

ONE OF THE BIGGEST DECORATING CHALLENGES arises when something old or vintage comes into your ultramodern home, or you fall in love with a new vase from IKEA that seems to have no relation to any of the pieces of antique furniture that you scavenged from your grandmother's attic. Hey, you can't help what (or whom) you fall in love with!

But these styles can work wonderfully together when you find something to unify them. Color? Shape? Texture? Theme?

When we moved into the Beekman farmhouse, we were perplexed by what to do with two of the small rooms that had originally been the servants' quarters.

One in particular wasn't big enough to accommodate a modern bed of any type, and to turn it into a closet or storage space seemed like a waste of a good window.

Instead, we turned it into a small study that we call the "writing room." We lined the walls with old portraits Brent had collected from his grandparents' antique frame business. Completely filling the wall space above the chair rail, the collection makes for a dramatic modern "gallery," and the room has become one of the most photographed in the house.

Everything old really can be new again if you only look at it in a new way.

> There is no difference between Time and any of the three dimensions of Space except that our consciousness moves along it. Scientific people . . . know very well that Time is only a kind of Space.
>
> —H. G. WELLS, *THE TIME MACHINE*, 1895

Opposite ~ The writing room at the Beekman Farm, with portraits.

Above ~ AT ONE POINT, drop ceilings and linoleum were au courant. But times and styles change. In this converted post office in Buffalo, Minnesota, the walls were stripped down to the bricks, a dropped ceiling was removed to reveal rafters, and the wood floor was painted white. A Louis XVI–style daybed, a 1920s pedestal table painted glossy white, and a linen-covered ottoman give this room a wonderful atmosphere.

Opposite ~ IN THE SAME CONVERTED BUILDING, the exposed lath makes a beautiful contrast to the ornate chandelier and plasterwork.

Above ~ Just because you have a simple cabin by the lake doesn't mean that every piece of furniture has to be made of twigs and bark. Here molded fiberglass chairs scooped up at the huge outdoor antiques festival in Brimfield, Massachusetts, offer a modern place to relax in a rustic setting.

Opposite ~ Every piece in this sitting area is old or repurposed, but the unique use of lace and the bold choice of color take it from fuddy-duddy to fabulous. Think about how you can build scenes like this from pieces you may have inherited.

Above ~ THIS KITCHEN BLENDS OLD AND NEW perfectly and delivers analog charm and function. This antique cabinet from an old hardware store influenced the design of the entire room. The kitchen island was built out of plywood to mask an undercounter refrigerator and dishwasher and then clad in Stikwood adhesive paneling and topped with zinc. This piece becomes the inspiration for the room rather than letting the appliances dominate. Is the burlap pendant lamp old or new? Check some back issues of the Restoration Hardware catalog for the answer. Notice the use of old apple crates for additional storage under the farmhouse sink.

Opposite ~ YOU MAY HAVE THE URGE to decorate this 1907 lodge in dark pieces to match the austerity of the surroundings, but here this übermodern Eero Saarinen table serves as a perfect break from the traditional. It's been artfully topped with a bust scored on Etsy and a mix and match of family heirlooms.

Following spread ~ THIS CACHE of small-scale 1950s looking glasses adds up to one sparkling focal point. The dark green paint and matching velvet settee fade into the background, while the loose symmetry creates an orderly, knockout effect. We are planning to use this same idea on one of the walls of the dining room in the Beekman farmhouse. We're collecting varying sizes of circular gilded eagle-topped mirrors.

Above ~ HANG AN OLD RUG OR QUILT to fashion a brand-new kind of headboard for your bed. This one dates to 1854 but, used in this fashion, looks very up-to-date.

Opposite ~ THINKING OF OLD THINGS IN A NEW WAY brings a fresh perspective to this dining nook. The aluminum pendant once lit an airplane hangar. If you saw this in an architectural salvage yard, you'd probably think it was too big for practical use, but as demonstrated here, it's not. The settee was reupholstered using US Mail bags.

You can easily create a whole new view from your porch. Upload your favorite snapshot (we like megaprint .com) and have it printed on weather-resistant vinyl. The banner comes to you complete with grommets for hanging.

Our own Beekman 1802 furniture collection is a blend of old textures and new silhouettes and careful plays on scale. In a similar fashion, we love how this very modern kitchen is anchored by the custom island that echoes the barnwood beams in the ceiling.

Sometimes all a room needs to make it stand out is an interesting new use for a traditional item, like the use of this well-worn rug instead of a regular bath mat.

The SECRET to this subtle yet super-stylish wall treatment? Ceiling medallions from the big-box hardware store! They were installed in a single day using adhesive caulk.

Above ~ WHEN WE RENOVATED the 150-year-old building that houses the flagship Beekman 1802 Mercantile, we painted the entire structure except the trim. We left it in the peeling shade of cream applied many years ago. We love the juxtaposition of something worn and rough with something smooth and shiny, and this room does it perfectly. The old plaster walls are made even more beautiful by the perfect lines of the window trim and the floor molding.

Opposite ~ Beekman 1802 Mercantile in Sharon Springs, New York.

Above ~ Sometimes it's the tiniest details. This bedroom is gorgeous as a whole, but one of the best ideas here is the contrast between the rough, untreated plank floors and the baseboard that has been painted in a high-gloss white. When you can't afford to refinish old wooden floors, make a statement about their worn condition with this type of contrast.

Opposite ~ At first glance, this looks like a very traditional dining room, but when you start to break down the elements, you'll see it's anything but. Mismatched chairs, a 1930s table, and a Noguchi paper lantern—all come together beautifully. What really makes this room work is the use of curved shapes, from the backs of the chairs to the light fixture to the doors on the built-in cabinet (accented by the wreath).

GOOD DESIGN can be done on the cheap. This kitchen
makeover came mostly from IKEA (cabinets, countertops,
and even the farmhouse sink). The antique bakery table
and its well-trodden wood floors add visual interest and
form the center of the room. All the new stuff just serves
as a frame.

How MANY TIMES have you seen a version of these twin beds? They are a staple of so many guest rooms, but look how easily you can give your guests something to write home about by adding a blingy mirrored desk (that doubles as a nightstand) and some generous pops of color.

In this attic guest room, big-box store bargains—a Room & Board bed frame, an IKEA cowhide rug, and a Lucite table from CB2—pair well with the English Regency table and 1970s mirror.

If you want a standout space, then you have to step outside the traditional decorating box. The peeling paint, the unique (and easy!) method of hanging artwork, and the partially painted Windsor bench make this room look very much of the moment.

DISPLAYING MULTIPLES of items in symmetrical rows
makes almost any collection seem modern. The key with
this technique is making sure that you have enough items
in the collection to fill the required space and make an
impact.

Above ~ In this 1920s house, railroad trestles were used as ceiling beams. A flea-market oil portrait watches over the antique iron bed, which is outfitted with bedding from Pottery Barn.

Following spread ~ Just because you are living in a single-story "dogtrot"-style house from the 1850s doesn't mean you have to abandon your love affair with the smooth lines of midcentury modern furniture. Here the walls and trim have been painted a high-gloss ebony, which throws the pale 1950s furniture into sharp relief.

ONE OF THE MOST PERFECT EXAMPLES of old meets new you are ever likely to see. New custom club sofas flank this family room's centerpiece—an oversize midcentury coffee table fashioned from iron and bleached oak. The twist-turned-leg chairs were found at an antiques store. The newly constructed shelving unit painted in a gloss white serves as the perfect setting for the patina provided by the collection of old ironstone.

Opposite ~ NEW FIBERGLASS CHAIRS by Modernica contrast with this dining room's 1870s Italian worktable (which is 11 feet long!). The 1960s glass lighting fixture was found at 1stdibs.com and the dress form at Urban Outfitters. The built-in cabinet (painted in Sea Wave Blue by Valspar) and the bird-themed wallpaper applied to the ceiling bring in a bit of whimsy that makes this room unforgettable.

Above ~ IF YOU LIKE A BOLD PATTERN, you don't have to limit yourself to one attention-grabbing accessory. In this living room, stripes are the ties that bind. If the room had *only* the curtains or *only* the rug, it wouldn't be that distinctive. By using corresponding patterns, you can show that the choices are deliberate. The striped chair looks like an expensive designer piece, but here the look was created by using upholstery paint found in any craft store.

FRUIT-PUNCH COLORS provide a vibrant foil to this kitchen's rustic beams and wood paneling. Even the vintage enamelware looks ultrachic when collected near the ceiling, proving that sometimes old things just need to be put into a new context to be seen in a more modern way. Case in point: The edges of the curtains were crocheted, showing this age-old handicraft in a completely new light.

There's almost nothing as old-fashioned as a rag rug, but stitching several together—now that is something completely new! If you can't sew, take the rugs to your local dry cleaner and have them join the mats.

An old idea, like these silhouettes rendered in a different material, scale, and format becomes suddenly fresher and more interesting. Silhouettes can be easily and cheaply made using pictures of children and pets or by doing a simple image search on the Internet.

JUST AS BRINGING in dramatic new color schemes can liven up a stale environment, an array of subtle textures and patterns can provide a needed visual spark, too. If you think you are not skilled enough to pull something like this off, break down the task. Find a few "common threads," like the stripes and the hints of red here, that can tie everything together.

When you are moving into a new home, money is often tight. But making your new place the envy of the neighborhood does not have to cost a fortune. None of the accessories in this room cost over $50. Combining two small side tables to fashion a larger surface to serve as a coffee table is creative thinking—which can save you lots of money.

SOMEONE WAS PAYING ATTENTION to everything we just said in this chapter!

The wallpaper was what inspired the makeover of this mere 12- by 13-foot room. The rich colors and large-scale pattern actually make the room feel more expansive while remaining intimate. The floor was painted, and even more pattern was brought into the room in the hooked rug and the striped silk curtains. Footstools were reupholstered in pink so they blend with the rest of the décor.

Chapter Two

BIG MEETS SMALL

M F_g F_g

d

$$F_g = \frac{GMm}{d^2}$$

Newton's law of universal gravitation states that any two bodies in the universe attract each other with a force that is directly proportional to the product of their masses and inversely proportional to the square of the distance between them. So a small object can only attract another small object that's nearby, but a large object, like a planet or a star, can pull in objects from across a vast distance.

Life is made up of moments. Big "statement" moments often receive the most attention, but precious little moments should not be forgotten either. The same can be said about designing your living spaces. Sure, pay attention to the foyer, but don't forget about the nook at the top of the stairs; small spaces can draw attention also.

On the main staircase in our home, there was a large, blank (and curved!) wall. For the first 3 years, we just ignored it. Then one day, Brent conjured a childhood memory. On long family road trips, the kids were given a "big book of puzzles." Among the crosswords, word searches, and anagrams were drawing exercises. On one page, you'd see a drawing of, say, the Mona Lisa. Then you would see the same drawing with a grid superimposed over it. Then you were given a blank grid. By focusing on drawing only the portion that occupied each grid, you ultimately created the big picture and surprised yourself with your artistic talent.

Don't be afraid to play with scale in your own home. One size rarely fits all, so don't hesitate to go big (or small).

Opposite ~ Silhouette paper artist Thom Mullins created this panoramic scene of the farm. Each frame is an individual work of art, but when they are all put together—it is a true masterpiece.

DISPLAYED BY THE DOZENS, a slapdash collection comes together harmoniously. You can find armfuls of bowls at places like restaurant supply stores, IKEA, or Pottery Barn and mix in vintage finds from garage sales, flea markets, and your own collection.

When working with a rustic form, match it with something a little more polished. Here the small pattern on the wallpaper serves as a great backdrop for a larger piece of furniture with a monotone but bright makeover. We use a big piece very similar to this as our checkout counter in the Beekman 1802 Mercantile flagship store.

Above ~ In this schoolhouse turned dwelling, a gymnastics pommel horse with its legs shortened serves as a bench in the mudroom. When you've got a big blank wall, don't be afraid to fill it with another large item (and it doesn't have to be a print or a mirror). Here a chalkboard was used—which is also a convenient place to leave messages.

Opposite ~ Sometimes we overlook small spaces when decorating, but these spaces can be used to provide extra visual interest. A collection of small picture frames serves as a great border to this built-in bookshelf. This is a clever way to display a collection without taking up too much space in the room.

HAVE A BIG SPACE TO FILL? Think of grouping objects of a
similar style or color. Here vintage sepia postcards were
affixed to a larger painter's canvas. The installation helps
give balance to the bright color of the wall behind it.

PEOPLE OFTEN THINK that if they have a really small space, they can't incorporate large objects. This is simply untrue, especially when the large pieces are functional. This oversize mirror—a vintage find from the 1800s— actually makes the room seem bigger and brighter.

Above ~ THIS CLEVER DISPLAY TWIST—a collection of small shelves for a collection of small items—uses up a large space by creating form as well as function.

Opposite ~ THINK OF A LARGE WALL like a big blank canvas. Sometimes you only need one item, and it works best when that one item is a conversation starter like this vintage biology chart. Notice how this works beautifully here, even though you might not necessarily have thought of using the chart if you ran across it at a yard sale.

418 BLASTODINIUM SPINULOSUM

BLASTODINIUM CRASSUM

Blow things up! A table runner that is beyond measure.

STEP ONE Cut a strip from a painter's drop cloth that measures 14¼ inches wide by 8 feet 1¼ inches long and press it to iron out any wrinkles. Create a ⅝-inch hem on all four sides.

STEP TWO Working on one of the strip's long sides and starting at a short end, use a ruler and a pencil to measure and mark 1 inch at a time; continue until you reach the other end. Repeat on the opposite side of the strip. Next, using your ruler, draw a line at each mark, varying the line lengths. At each 16th mark, draw a line that crosses the entire strip as you can see above. Trace over the lines using a black fabric marker.

STEP THREE Affix a 6-inch-high number stencil using stencil adhesive.

STEP FOUR Using a foam brush, fill in the stencil with fabric paint.

STEP FIVE After the paint dries (about 1 hour), spray the runner with Scotchgard fabric protector, which will help keep it clean and allow for spot treating small spills.

A COLLECTION of small tramp art frames asymmetrically mounted makes for a visually interesting way to fill the space above a sofa. This is where a lot of people go wrong by hanging something too small in the dead center of the wall above the furniture.

Above left and right ~ Blow it up! Oversize clocks.

Right ~ Blow it up! This incredible wall art was created by having a local copy center enlarge a cross-stitch pattern that was then stenciled directly onto the wall. From a distance, the image is apparent, but up close you have a modern work of art.

Opposite ~ One large, dramatic print is sometimes all you need in a small room. Use minimal décor for maximum impact. This curtain is by designer Thomas Paul, but you could easily make this yourself using readily available clip art. Simply find the image you like by doing a Google search, and then use an online poster-printing service.

CHAPTER THREE

BLACK MEETS WHITE

PEOPLE OFTEN ASK us the key to our successful long-term relationship. We tell them that it's our differences that make us compatible. The same idea applies to finding a successful relationship between the objects in your home. In this chapter, we will show you how to utilize color contrast to make a dramatic statement in any room. Black-and-white focal points will be highlighted, but you'll also see examples of how other pops of unexpected color can be the singular element that any room needs.

When we first moved into Beekman Farm, the large rooms were framed at floor and ceiling with gorgeous hand-carved molding. Perhaps ornate by modern standards, it serves as a stirring juxtaposition to the clean lines of some of our more modern furniture choices. However, notice how modern patterns (like the textile on the sofas) were used on a piece of furniture with a more classic silhouette. An antique gilded mirror became a focal point when we had our local auto shop powder-coat it in shiny orange paint (opposite).

With these additions, the formal living room keeps its formality without looking stuffy or pretentious. Through contrast, we achieved harmony.

Newton's color circle (1704) displayed seven colors. He declared that colors opposite each other had the strongest contrast and harmony.

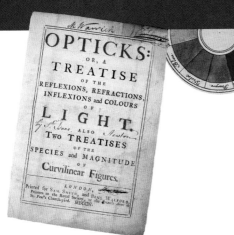

Opposite ~ A shot of the living room at Beekman Farm.

Opposite—IF YOU HAVE EVER LIVED in a rented home, you know that the walls are often painted in a neutral color that you can't change. But that doesn't mean you can't have a statement-making room. All you need is some dark furniture and accessories. Since you'll take them with you if you move, you can go ahead and invest in antique or higher-quality pieces that will last a lifetime.

Above—THIS OVERSIZE TIN MONOGRAM (originally from a gas station sign) stands out against the hand-pickled pine walls. The contrast really updates this living room in a 1960s ranch house.

Opposite ~ NEUTRAL HUES UNITE the variety of vintage chairs surrounding this dining table. Painting the table white shows off the curves of the legs and creates a stunning contrast to the dark wood of the floor and cabinetry.

Above ~ THE SHADES OF WHITE and just a few pops of dark in this collection (even the use of shadows and joints) make it much more visually interesting.

Above ~ DECORATING MOSTLY with black and white gives you the freedom to bring in whimsical bits of color. This simple cotton rug with a red stripe from IKEA becomes a standout in this room.

Opposite ~ A COLLAGE OF FAMILY PHOTOS in simple black frames against a white wall creates as much visual interest as a highly patterned wallpaper.

As THEY SAY, it's not always black and white. Sometimes shades of gray (like these chairs) and even the dark golden color of the light fixture fashioned from reclaimed oyster sticks can provide nice contrast.

This KITCHEN from the same house (opposite) uses an
antique crock as a trash or compost receptacle.
The interior is painted black, which references the same
lines and tones in the hanging lamps. Attention to details
like this can really pull the room together visually.

IF YOU ARE ONE OF THOSE PEOPLE who just love color and a black-and-white environment is not for you, you can get the same impact using light colors and dark furnishings like this set of vintage chairs, which pop against the pastel wall.

If you want to do something a little different, try the other way around. Paint the walls a dark color and let lighter pieces of furniture shine.

SOMETIMES YOU HAVE TO go all the way! If we've convinced you of the merits of black-and-white contrast in your home—we mean really convinced—consider this bold approach. This sort of treatment is perfect in a small room like a foyer or entry hallway where you want to give guests their first hint of how fabulous you are.

OFTEN WHEN DECORATING with high contrasts, it's all about silhouette and form. A black wrought-iron light fixture and ebony gateleg table transform this screened-in back porch into an ideal dining room. The black elements are wonderfully silhouetted against the sunny exterior.

Above ~ In this small kitchen, full upper cabinets would have made the space claustrophobic. Simple white planks and custom brackets set against a chalkboard-painted wall keep things light. Notice how the lines of the appliances and even the water pitcher relate to the larger design elements in the room.

Following spread ~ In this living room of mostly neutrals and whites, the dark surround on the fireplace becomes the focal point of the room.

Black on black. Imagine this bathroom with a standard
white pedestal sink. The wallpaper would not have the
same effect if the pop of extra black were not on the base
of the sink. In this case, the black-and-white wallpaper
becomes more of a neutral background and allows the
sink to stand out.

THINGS DON'T ALWAYS have to be high contrast to create the desired effect. This wall transitions from white on the bottom to the aged newsprint on the top. The brown table brings out the golden color of the paper and the floor. And it all comes together to serve as an appealing background for the handsome hutch.

THIS ARRESTING WALLPAPER by designer Sheila Bridges is made more powerful by the black cabinet and the white mirror that give the eyes a place to rest.

ARE YOU NOTICING A THEME? Sometimes just an element of black-and-white contrast can bring out the beauty of neutral tones. Sometimes a little makes a lot of difference. This arrow print wallpaper from cavernhome.com points the way to a look that is at once minimal and bold.

Above and opposite ~ THESE CERAMIC DESIGNS from artist Laura Zindel were the inspiration for her own home's décor! All of the furniture was crafted in a local Amish community, but the use of contrast gives this room a decidedly urban feel.

Opposite ~ A STACK OF UKRAINIAN NEWSPAPERS from the 1960s was purchased at a Pennsylvania flea market for $20. With wallpaper paste and flat craft sealant, the walls become an incredible backdrop for the stark white sink. Even the electrical outlet looks like a well-placed piece of art!

Above ~ A FUTURE BEEKMAN BOY (with his first pair of Muck Boots and everything!) is already learning how to make an entrance. Here black and white set against a neutral background really distinguishes the key architectural feature of this area of the home.

Above ~ How often have you seen an old checkerboard linoleum floor and thought that there was just no way to decorate around it? Here's proof that it can be done and can be fabulous!

Opposite ~ People often think that "decorating" a room is only about the objects that you put on some sort of flat surface. But in this dining area, it's the dark vertical and horizontal lines of the cabinets, the bar, and even the iron ladder that create the real visual interest.

We love this collection of English ironstone and less expensive white pottery and glass. Painting the interior of the built-in cabinet a dark gray makes this collection a true standout.

You CAN HAVE A GREAT ROOM on the cheap by using contrast. This guest bedroom is fairly minimal when it comes to decoration. The elaborate bed silhouetted against the light walls is all the ornamentation the room needs.

Above and opposite ~ WHAT COULD HAVE BEEN just a passage-way went from drab to a fab and functional dining room using black and white. Inexpensive Windsor chairs, slat-back benches from Crate & Barrel, and simple forged-iron chandeliers unite to create a great look.

Above ~ CREATE YOUR OWN DRAMA! Using tape or tacks, secure vintage doilies to the glass or open backs of black frames. Place on a dark-hued wall.

Opposite ~ DESIGNER TRACY REESE knows how to create stunning dresses for the likes of Taylor Swift and Michelle Obama, and she knows how to create a stunning room using darks and lights.

Like a scene right out of Beekman Farm, this simple
tableau lacks nothing in style.

THIS IS OUR DREAM KITCHEN! The dark cabinets were inspired by the stove, but it all seems to disappear as the eye is drawn to the windows and the view. This brings up another important point. Sometimes black, especially large areas of it, can create a void to draw the eye away from an area that you don't want people to focus on and can even mask less desirable architectural features by making them fade into the background.

The DARK AND WARM PAINT COLOR in this office space sets off not only the white trim but also the metallic accents in the room. The color is a great alternative when you don't want to go all the way to black.

BEFORE

Above ~ THIS MAKEOVER had a budget of $15,000. Here's how it was done. On the following page, you can see the "after." The results are (practically) priceless.

STEP ONE Add instant character overhead. Rather than rip down the flimsy fiberboard ceiling, it was covered in affordable sheets of bead-board paneling. The seams were disguised using two-by-fours that mimic the look of exposed beams.

STEP TWO Open the door to another opportunity. The French door with a Colonial style gives the room an updated look.

STEP THREE Put old cabinetry in a new context. Replacing the kitchenette's Formica counters with butcher block counters from IKEA completely transforms the look of the room from dated to farmhouse chic.

STEP FOUR Nothing a coat of paint can't fix. The floors were a mismatched and not particularly attractive wood. Painted a soft gray using porch paint, the faults are masked and the focus of the room becomes the other dark elements like the pendant light fixture and the fireplace screen.

STEP FIVE Old style up in smoke: A faux fireplace with electric logs that don't require chimney ventilation looks like it was always a part of the room.

AFTER

CHAPTER FOUR

UP MEETS DOWN

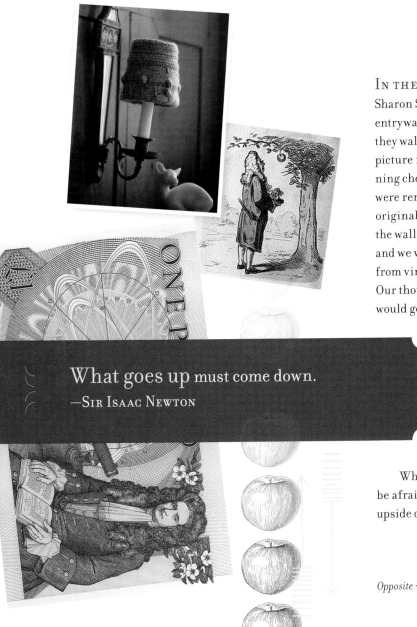

IN THE FLAGSHIP BEEKMAN 1802 MERCANTILE in Sharon Springs, New York, we wanted to create a dramatic entryway that would delight our customers the moment they walked in the door. We achieved this by using strips of picture frame molding (and a miter saw) to create a stunning chevron pattern down the length of the hallway. We were renovating an old building that still had some of the original tin ceilings. After spending so much money on the walls, we couldn't afford pressed tin for the ceiling, and we went with much more affordable faux tin tiles made from vinyl (you can get these at the big-box home stores). Our thought was that the ceilings were so high that no one would get close enough to tell the difference.

We loved the look of the tiles and the ease of installing them so much that we then decided to cover an entire vertical wall with them. To add an extra layer of detail and dimension, we used upholstery tacks to cover the seams between the square tiles. The final look is luxe, even though it was created on a strict budget.

When shopping for supplies for home projects, don't be afraid to get creative. It might just turn your world upside down.

> **What goes up** must come down.
> —SIR ISAAC NEWTON

Opposite ~ The entry hall at Beekman 1802 Mercantile.

HERE SWATCHES of Indian bedding were used to upholster
an old dresser to create a stunning tableau.

Up the down staircase! Hanging small pieces of artwork or photographs on a staircase riser can provide unexpected visual appeal—turning an overlooked surface into a real focal point.

Painted stripes on the ceiling bring additional verve to this bedroom. To create the tone-on-tone stripes, choose two cans of the same color of paint and ask the paint store to dilute one by 50 percent.

PLANKS FROM AN OLD BARN FLOOR become shelves, and an old metal awning conceals the ventilation duct in this kitchen.

Above ~ Cow feed sifters were lined with burlap to make these sconces, and planks from Habitat for Humanity's ReStore line the sitting-room ceiling.

Opposite ~ Wallpaper used on the walls in an adjacent room covers the ceiling in this one, creating a natural, if unorthodox, design flow through the house.

THIS IS A GORGEOUS KITCHEN ISLAND fashioned from reclaimed wood, but the real stroke of genius here is the roman shade over the kitchen sink. It was constructed from an old tablecloth.

For a small fixture with tons of texture.

STEP ONE Cut a knit swatch from an old or unwanted sweater to wrap around your shade, adding an extra ½ inch to the top and bottom.

STEP TWO Hot-glue the fabric to the shade so that it meets in the back.

STEP THREE Tuck the excess material over the top and the bottom edges and glue into place.

Above ~ In this kitchen, the backsplash goes from blah to beautiful by using faux bois floor tiles on the wall. The nautical rope light pendant is by Atelier 688.

Following spread ~ The dramatic floor-sweeping curtains in this dining room were fashioned from a humble painter's drop cloth.

HERE'S ONE WAY TO SHUTTER out a boring wall.

STEP ONE Measure the wall you plan to cover.

STEP TWO Go on a hunt to your local salvage yard or home supply store or look online to find enough shutters to cover the space. Remove any hardware.

STEP THREE Mark off a space on the floor or in your yard that corresponds to the wall's dimensions. Within that area, play with the placement of the shutters, marking where to cut any that overlap. Once satisfied with the arrangement, mark each shutter with a number keyed to a paint color to ensure a varied palette.

STEP FOUR Cut the marked shutters and sand the edges and then paint. To give some shutters an aged look, apply a dark ebony stain over the dry paint and then wipe off the stain after about 30 seconds.

STEP FIVE Create a support system by cutting strips of ⅝-inch plywood and nailing them to the wall to bridge the gap between studs. Do this down the height of the wall, separating each strip by about 18 inches.

STEP SIX Placing one shutter at a time, put each into position on the wall.

If you've used several corresponding colors throughout the house, this is a good way to use up leftover paint and tie all of your home's colors together in one dramatic spot.

THE BEAUTIFUL CURTAINS in this dining room were created by stitching together classic Hudson's Bay wool blankets, and the table was given an edgy look by replacing its traditional Colonial-style legs with portions of old utility poles.

Above ~ Steel plumbing pipes attached to the ceiling create a wonderfully inventive chandelier. There are endless possibilities of things you could hang from the structure to create an overhead lighting source that is truly unique to your room.

Opposite ~ An old chicken crate makes a coffee-table base with rustic appeal.

CHAPTER FIVE

EAST MEETS WEST

THE AGE OF EXPLORATION was driven by man's desire to see "the other side of the world"—literally. It was that same sense of exploration that drew us out of Manhattan and to the farmlands of upstate New York.

When we moved into the house, the prior owners had spent a small fortune installing hand-printed wallpaper throughout. The two center hallways are adorned with a dramatic pale green and antiqued gold chinoiserie design. We may have never chosen this pattern, but we have fallen in love with how it sits against the things that we brought into the house.

The lessons here are twofold.

First, don't assume that items with an ethnic or more "global" feel won't work in your home. If you love something, you can find a way to make it work.

Second, when you move into a new house, you may not have the financial resources to undo the work of the prior owners. Don't let this deter you. Sometimes the most brilliant combinations come from being exposed to layout and design challenges you would have never otherwise thought of.

Just keep reminding yourself of the fact that polar opposites can lead to a truly magnetic attraction.

> Magnetism was originally used not for navigation but for fortune-telling by the Chinese. The earliest Chinese magnetic compasses were probably not designed for navigation but rather to order and harmonize their environments and buildings in accordance with the geomantic principles of feng shui.

Opposite ~ East meets West in a corner of Brent and Josh's home.

Opposite ~ Imagine this room without the wall covering. The individual pieces would be fairly mundane, but the opulent wallpaper (from Waverly) makes an Eastern statement that is brought home by painting the cane-backed chairs a glossy fire-engine red.

Above ~ This pared-down room is simplicity at its finest: a watchmaker's desk from the 1890s combined with an antique barbershop chair and an old mirror. Is there anything else you need to sit down and write the next great novel?

Above ~ A BATHROOM (especially a small one) can be difficult to keep "clean and simple," but it's accomplished here with an above-counter Giove sink from Scarabeo and gray marble subway tiles from Walker Zanger.

Opposite ~ THIS RUSTIC COUNTRY PORCH seems like the last place you'd find worlds colliding, but this powder-coated and lightweight steel side table (from worldmarket.com) painted in a vibrant coral red creates a whole new view.

Above ~ EAST REALLY DOES MEET WEST in this bathroom with a modern Japanese-influenced pedestal sink paired with a marble-topped and painted cabinet that has the decorative flare of the French.

Opposite ~ IN THIS "WOW MOMENT" ENTRYWAY, the wallpaper, the woven baskets, the pendant light, and the pottery take the mind to the Orient, but it's all brought back home by pairing these elements with the cabinets lined with chicken wire. You'll recognize this wallpaper from page 99.

THE LINES AND FLOW of this dining room make it a room you'll want to do more than eat in. The wallpaper is from Schumacher. Reminiscent of traditional paper cutting, it feels both modern and old-fashioned and actually negates the need for any wall art. Notice how the round table by Ballard Designs softens the room's right angles, while Crate & Barrel's white bentwood chairs provide contrast. These are feng shui principles at their best.

THE NAUTICAL INFLUENCES in this bedroom redesign are unmistakable, but look how nicely they exist with the simple patterned rug.

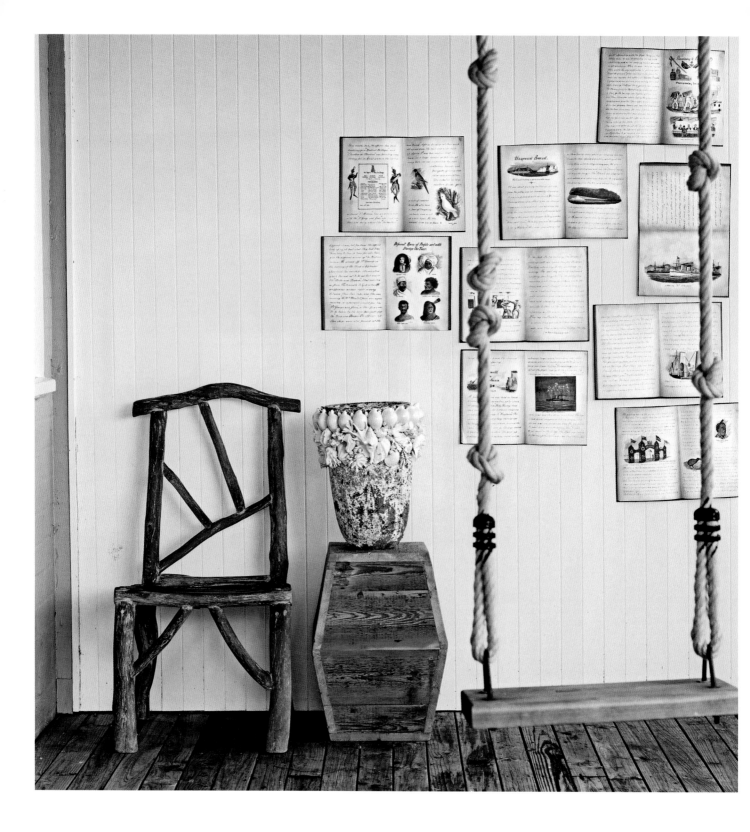

Above ~ CRACK A BOOK and create a gallery. Rather than merely photocopying or scanning a found image, use an entire open book. You can pin the pages to the wall in various arrangements to give it a "today's lesson" feel.

Opposite ~ THIS DINING ROOM'S MYRIAD TREASURES speak to world-traveler wannabes. An Italian chandelier, a mid-century Parsons table clad in bird's-eye maple veneer, and a Louis XVI–style mirror show that even a taste for the exotic can be brought together in a tasteful way.

You can accomplish an Asian aesthetic without making much commitment at all. Here it's done with some simple accessories from nature. The best thing about this sort of arrangement is that there's absolutely no arranging involved. The leaves have been stripped before putting the limb in the vase, highlighting the prettiest feature of the plant—its fruit. This was done with crab apple branches, but you could also try figs, chestnuts, or lady apples.

THIS GUEST BEDROOM captures the look of an East Coast summer cottage in a wealthy second-home community. You can easily find lamps and other accessories by searching eBay and Etsy for terms like "Asian" or "blanc de chine."

Toile, lacquer, and gold all together? Yes. Enough said.

Though this ceramic stove is from Italy, painted in a bright yellow hue, it reminds us of a pagoda where one would go to meditate on the sunny influences of this room.

Above ~ THIS HUTCH SET AGAINST A WALL painted black would look equally as enticing in a Chinese teahouse as it does in this room in a remodeled farmhouse.

Opposite ~ AN OVERSIZE MIRROR creates the illusion of an entrance to another room. Mauve velvet updates an Empire sofa found at a local antiques shop. The wallpaper is from Cole & Son, and the overall effect looks like the French Concession in Shanghai.

SOMETIMES THE SUBTLE LINES of a single piece of furniture can influence the design direction of a room—like the pagoda silhouette of this headboard.

THE QUICKEST WAY to add charm and character is with
wallpaper. In this bedroom, the lines of the headboard
and the birdcage pattern on the walls unexpectedly pair
well with gingham, toile, and plaid.

CHAPTER SIX

FORM MEETS FUNCTION

WHEN WE LIVED IN NEW YORK CITY, it was easy to eschew the myriad of fancy antiques shops for the architectural salvage store or the industrial supply shops of Canal Street or the outer boroughs.

If something was rusty or dusty or had some chipping paint, we loved it ever so much more.

This love of the well-worn and well-used workhorses from both agrarian and industrial environs shines through in the furniture we design for our collection. We think something is even more beautiful for the fact that it functions as well as it fills a space.

Perfect form can create a timelessly beautiful object and precision function, a degree of necessity. A little creative spark between the two—like metal striking metal—forges something completely unforgettable.

> The whole is greater than the sum of its parts.
> —ARISTOTLE

Opposite ~ When we design pieces for the Beekman 1802 Heirloom Collection, we strive to find the perfect balance between form and function: a blend of industrial pragmatism and romantic idealism.

Above ~ WE LOVE THE IDEA of having a bench in the mudroom, but that doesn't mean you have to sacrifice style.
This two-seater bench is from the 19th century, but you
can create something similar on your own by finding two
identical armless dining chairs, attaching them side by
side, painting them, and then placing one long cushion
across the two seats.

Opposite ~ DATING FROM THE 1930s through the '50s, these
valises add up to a stunning side table—one that also
provides off-season clothing storage.

This 2- by 6-foot closet was transformed into a functional workspace blooming with inspiration. Luxurious design choices—floral wallpaper, a beaded chandelier—make the small nook feel like a full-fledged room, while smart storage solutions maximize every square inch.

Avoid the visual clutter of brackets and other hardware by using floating plank shelves.

The desk was made using a melamine desktop and two standard metal file cabinets painted with spray paint.

ATTIC SPACES can have difficult angles to work around, but here the eaves become an ultracozy sleeping nook framed by the wood beams of the house. It becomes a private hideaway with the addition of a simple tension rod and inexpensive curtains.

Opposite ~ SOMETIMES YOU WANT a large and dramatic centerpiece but don't have the large and dramatic vessels you might need to pull it off. That's when it's time to get crafty. Here nine vintage milk bottles were tied together, proving once again that the sum is greater than the parts.

Above ~ THESE OLD HIGH SCHOOL lab microscopes (that we constantly see on eBay for as low as $50) have a wonderful industrial feel to them. We love their use here as bookends.

This NEW USE FOR AN OLD GLOBE will have your room glowing and brighten your worldview.

To make your own, you'll need:

~ A 12-inch-diameter cardboard globe

~ A pendant light cord kit

STEP ONE Remove your globe from its base, if necessary.

STEP TWO With a utility knife, carefully make a 3½-inch-diameter opening at the bottom of the globe using the latitude lines as a guide.

STEP THREE Holding the light cord's socket at the top of the globe, trace around it with a pencil and cut out the resulting circle.

STEP FOUR (Optional) Using a drill fitted with a ⅛-inch bit, pierce small holes around the outline of each continent, leaving ¼ inch between holes.

STEP FIVE Insert the socket at the top following the kit's instructions.

You COULD GO BROKE trying to fill a big centerpiece-size vase. Or use this strategy instead. Set a few small bottles inside a larger container, and suddenly a handful of single stems makes a huge impact.

Above ~ Come across a collection of vintage hangers or have too many in your closet? They become an elegant and practical way to hang guest towels (and provide guests with an extra place to hang clothes!).

Opposite ~ A functional (if rather plain) lampshade is given a designer redo by gluing paint sticks onto its surface. Go modern by dipping the sticks asymmetrically into paint or more rustic by leaving them unfinished.

WHEN SEVERAL PEOPLE share one bathroom, getting ready and out the door on time in the morning can be a challenge. This collection of vintage mirrors solves that problem while creating visual appeal and more light in a small room.

The 3-d effect of this project creates a mini work of art for each guest.

Here's how to do it:

STEP ONE Cut the silk flower from its stem and trim the backside so that it lies flat.

STEP TWO Experiment with flower placement on the left side of the mats. Once you're satisfied with the arrangements, use chalk to sketch a stem, leaves, or a branch. Mark where each flower will go, then set the flowers aside.

STEP THREE Using a needle and green or brown embroidery floss, follow the chalk marks with running stitches.

STEP FOUR Attach the flowers with large nylon snaps (available on Amazon.com). At each marked spot, hand-stitch the socket part of a snap onto the placemat. Next, hot-glue the ball part of the snap to the underside of the flower. Let dry for 3 minutes before snapping the flower onto the placemat. (Note: Simply snap off each flower before dry-cleaning or washing the mats by hand.)

Two become one! Two vintage side tables on casters function as a flexible alternative to the usual hulking coffee table.

A ZEBRA-PRINT OTTOMAN sidles up to a cast-iron tub in this beautiful master bathroom. We love the mirrors attached to a barn-door slide that open to reveal a recessed medicine cabinet and storage area.

Opposite ~ WE COULDN'T TALK about form meeting function without calling out this piece of work by Pennsylvania craftsman Brad Smith. Here he has turned ax handles and a pitchfork into sly seating (bradfordwoodworking.com).

Above ~ MOST PEOPLE have long since traded in CDs for digital downloads, but we hoard our relics of another age. Rather than tossing those plastic covers in the trash—most aren't recyclable—mount them on your walls! Blow up a favorite photo and then cut it into squares the size to fit each case.

You wouldn't think much could be done with an individual handheld mirror, but look how surrounding a portrait with a collection of them scales up the space, creating a whole wall of art.

CHAPTER SEVEN

IN MEETS OUT

WHEN WE FIRST MOVED TO OUR RURAL OUTPOST in Sharon Springs, we had visions of becoming one with nature, and to a very large extent this happened. The land, the environment, and the seasons began to dictate nearly every aspect of our life—from what we ate to what we wore to the products we designed. What was going on outside of our doors was so compelling that we couldn't help but let it influence how we designed our home.

For the downstairs hallway, we wanted a long narrow table that could fill that large space in a minimal way but also serve as an overflow dining or buffet area when we were entertaining large crowds.

Taking some vintage outdoor iron and brass table bases, we worked with our local blacksmith to create a 9-foot-long, 3-foot-wide zinc-clad table that stretches the length of the hallway. The zinc will patina beautifully over time, and the reflective surface brightens up the dark center of the room.

tro·pism /ˈtrōpizəm/ *noun*
1. the turning of all or part of an organism in a particular direction in response to an external stimulus.

Opposite ~ The entry hall at Beekman Farm.

Opposite ~ THIS HOME IS DECORATED for the Scandinavian Saint Lucia's Day holiday, and we love the warm, golden tones that the shafts of wheat bring to this dining table. When making centerpieces, don't be afraid to experiment with flora that is not typically seen as decorative.

Above ~ A 70-YEAR-OLD CLAM-SHUCKING TABLE, once used in an Atlantic City seafood restaurant, now serves as a plant stand in the dining room. Potting tables make beautiful pieces of furniture when you bring them indoors. Placed under a sunny window, they can become your very own indoor garden patch.

GARDEN STATUARY, especially pieces that have already marked several seasons outdoors, can make beautiful accent pieces in almost any room.

Above ~ ALWAYS DREAMED OF A HOUSE with a white picket fence? Making a picket-fence headboard will make that dream come true. Sort of.

Following spread ~ THIS OLD BARN becomes an indoor/ outdoor entertaining area with the addition of a concrete slab. During inclement weather, the tables and chairs are simply moved back inside.

At the end of summer, you can often find really good deals on outdoor furniture—and look how charming these metal chairs look around this dining table in this rustic cabin.

This PARTICULAR BIRCH LOUNGER graced the promenade deck of the *Queen Mary* in the 1950s! Passengers paid extra to sit on one, and reservations were placed in the metal plate on the arm. Pieces of outdoor furniture can work beautifully when brought indoors.

We love how the outdoor firewood stand in the corner of this den brings a bit of the outdoors into an otherwise basic room in a sculptural way. Some of the very best design comes from figuring out a clever way to disguise functional necessities of living.

Above left ~ OLD WICKER PORCH FURNITURE fits in beautifully in this sun-faded kitchen.

Above right ~ SIMILARLY, THIS PORCH has been enclosed to create an additional indoor living space, but the sturdy outdoor furniture looks just as good in the more sheltered setting.

Opposite ~ A SUNNY SPOT in this kitchen was the perfect place for a faux bois birdbath basin to corral some potted ferns. A mini herb garden would be lovely, too.

We call this the butterfly effect. Capture a Victorian cabinet-of-curiosities vibe—minus all the hunting and gathering—by using faux butterflies.

To create this look:

STEP ONE Find a glass dome at a craft or home and garden store.

STEP TWO Using a serrated knife, cut a 1-inch-thick piece of Styrofoam into a circle that will fit the base of the dome.

STEP THREE Next, cut a piece of black velvet with a large enough diameter to cover the top and sides of the Styrofoam. Pull the fabric over the foam circle until taut and affix underneath with straight pins.

STEP FOUR Cut pieces of 22-gauge wire to various heights that fit the dome. Place a dot of superglue on one wire before sliding it into the butterfly's body.

STEP FIVE Finally, insert the wires into the Styrofoam base, then top with the glass dome.

An INDUSTRIAL WORKTABLE, topped with custom-cut glass, serves as the kitchen island. A vintage icebox came in from the cold to offer hidden storage, while rough-hewn Douglas fir shelves hold dishes and cookware. The perfect blend of outdoors and indoors.

The lamp in this room was fashioned after an old
weathervane.

There are so many kinds of beds, but we love this
Adirondack-style hickory bed. It really brings a bit of
nature into the room.

To MAKE THIS handy outdoor bar cart, remove the wheels and axles from vintage toy red wagons of roughly the same size. For the bottom shelf, attach galvanized floor flanges on the inside four corners with nuts and bolts. Mount casters to the underside. For the middle shelf, attach two floor flanges (one on the inside, one on the bottom) in all four corners with nuts and bolts. For the top shelf, attach galvanized floor flanges on the bottom four corners with nuts and bolts. Next, use screws and liquid nails to adhere 12-inch-long wooden dowels to the center of the flanges to build one unified structure.

The STARK WHITE WALLS and the thick, modern lines of the dark table become even more interesting when contrasted with the scraped, beaten, and chipped bench and chair.

WHAT LOOKS LIKE AN OLD PICNIC TABLE is the grounding
element of this room. It's actually an old military-cot bed
frame topped with reclaimed barn wood.

This swinging bed looks equally enticing on a porch or in a bedroom.

Above ~ Sᴇᴀ ɢʀᴀss ᴀʀᴍᴄʜᴀɪʀs and ottoman blend interior comfort with outdoorsy charm.

Opposite ~ Vᴇʀᴛɪᴄᴀʟ ɢᴀʀᴅᴇɴs are all the rage, and you can make your own wall-mounted herb garden for tableside snipping.

Above ~ An old DAYBED placed beneath a tree and covered with an outdoor furniture pad will become a favorite spot to while away the hours or contemplate a new project.

Opposite ~ An old ZINC BISTRO TABLE gets some fabulous dining partners with these chairs painted in a bold fuchsia.

Opposite ~ Bringing the outdoors inside can be taken literally. A fallen tree was painted white and serves as a stunning centerpiece in this kitchen.

Above ~ You can take the outdoors in, but the indoors can also go out. While this furniture will not last as long when exposed to the elements, it will patina beautifully and you'll still get years of use from it. This is a great way to utilize hand-me-down wooden furniture that doesn't fit in your home.

Above ~ THIS LIBRARY'S 12-FOOT-LONG TABLE and built-in bookshelves were made using bark-on birch trunks.

Opposite ~ OUTDOOR FURNITURE, CHECK. Indoor plants, check. This wonderful family room sums up every idea presented in this section. And there's not a single thing here that you couldn't accomplish in your own home.

CHAPTER EIGHT

HIGH MEETS LOW

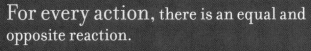

OPPOSITES ATTRACT because too many similar things together become monotonous and boring. The signature look of Beekman 1802 is the blend of the inexpensive and the exquisite. It's an aesthetic that developed naturally rather than deliberately. We've always been conscious consumers, laboring over (and often talking ourselves out of) the purchase of anything that comes into our home.

The result of such "discriminating taste" is that the items that we did splurge on hold a special place in our heart and in a room. If you rush to decorate a room just to get it "done," the end result is often a bit matchy-matchy. We'd rather have a space that's in progress than one filled with things that work together but lack the spark that makes a room memorable and lovable.

Just like you, we often look at catalogs like Crate & Barrel, Anthropologie, and Restoration Hardware for inspiration. The object-rich photos make each room seem voluptuous. It's important to remember that the job of the catalog is to sell product. Take these shots as inspiration, but rest assured that a room so full of stuff is no place to rest. Editing is where the best interior designers excel.

The risk of having too many splendid things is that they become less special.

> For every action, there is an equal and opposite reaction.
> —NEWTON'S THIRD LAW

Opposite ~ High meets low in the master bedroom of the Beekman Farm.

PLAY AGAINST TYPE. The paneling and wall of French doors
in this room could have made you lean toward a more
stuffy décor, but by painting the walls white and bringing
in comfortable furniture in shades of blue and gray, what
could have been an Old World library looks more like a
garden sunroom.

Nothing captures the high/low concept better than French Country style. The elegant (but worn) fainting couch and the French doors add a bit of panache to the painted plank floors and the comfy bed.

Above ~ The rustic fireplace in this 200-year-old house in Connecticut becomes the focal point of the room when surrounded by more elegant furniture. Every element has a well-used and well-loved patina. This is what we call aging gracefully.

Opposite ~ This dining room manages to escape looking too country by having a few moments of sparkle (the pewter set) and a moment of flare (in the painted cup chandelier). The nonfussy window treatment also plays a role.

SIMPLE WHITEWARE mixed with vintage red transferware
and displayed on open shelves in this kitchen provides
easy access. The addition of the silver serving pieces and
the casually propped oil paintings brings a little unexpected formality and visual interest.

STACKING CHAIRS from Donghia add contemporary contrast to the checked tablecloth in this dining room, making even something as country and traditional as gingham look fresh and modern.

This bedroom offers a lesson in mixing old and new. A grand 1940s bed, a pair of ornate 1920s English oak corner chairs, and turn-of-the-20th-century side tables are paired with crisp white bed linens and a pair of brushed nickel lamps from HomeGoods. Just because you inherit a suite of antiques doesn't mean you have to play to the period.

The antique chaise longue is matched here with a pillow from C. Wonder and a paisley wallpaper from Sanderson. The floral painting is a thrift-store discard.

Opposite ~ In this living room, a galvanized metal counter purchased for $100 brings the antique Louis XVI–style settee into a new setting. Perhaps this is just perfect for eating cake.

Above ~ Know when to splurge. Mixing a few big-ticket items among bargains makes everything look rich. Here a sturdy prep table picked up at an auction for $8 sits beneath an ornate iron chandelier that cost well over $1,000.

Above ~ DESIGNER CAMILLA FABBRI had a stroke of genius when she came up with this project. Using a cheap cylindrical vase, she spaced two rows of rubber bands around it and then tucked paintbrushes of various heights inside the bands until the tools completely surrounded the vessel. The effect is a vase that's as elegant as it is whimsical.

Opposite ~ FATHER-AND-DAUGHTER DUO Barry and Scarlett Scales take the fussiness out of period pieces by wrapping timeworn tables in zinc scraps rescued from old buildings near their hometown of Franklin, Tennessee (scarlettscales.com).

Opposite ~ A CUSTOM SOFA and a 1920s mirrored coffee table decorate this living room. The overhead light fixture was created from an old garden ornament.

Above ~ AN INDUSTRIAL STEEL-PIPE TABLE is dressed up with a huge slab of marble.

Above ~ Now this is farmhouse chic! None of the pieces in this living room was overly expensive, but the placement of the art makes it feel as if you stepped into a designer showroom.

Opposite ~ Highly styled pieces are more approachable (and exceptionally beautiful) when they carry ages of use. An 18th-century wooden angel looks over a simple pine trestle table, oak bistro chairs, and a slightly rusty wood-and-iron chandelier.

Above ~ In this master bathroom, a new tub by Water-works sits next to an antique table and a milking stool. A castoff window frame fitted with custom-cut mirrors becomes an impressive full-length looking glass.

Opposite ~ This enlarged map mounted on a three-panel wooden screen and an engraved silver coffee set bring a bit of bling to the entryway of this farmhouse.

WINGBACK CHAIRS upholstered in cotton and burlap complement a French-style sofa. The coffee table was fashioned by cutting a farm table down to size and then painting it a warm gray. A wooden stool found in a thrift shop serves as an interesting easel for a piece of art.

Opposite ~ IN THIS KITCHEN, a Murano glass chandelier offers a glamorous counterpoint to the hardworking antique oak island and industrial sink beneath.

Above ~ EMBRACE IMPERFECT ORIGINAL details when you live in an old house. A spare decorating approach can even enhance them. In this dining room, a mid-1800s portrait feels apropos against the room's original wood paneling. But steel bistro chairs deliver a jolt of modernism.

This is actually a very plain room, devoid of any architectural flourishes, and that sets the stage for more luxurious furnishings like these corduroy-upholstered wing
chairs. The fireplace had no decorative carving or plasterwork, but this garland of dried magnolia leaves does
the trick.

GO FOR BAROQUE! Recast in creamy whites, ornate frippery reveals a minimalist side. Here Victorian door sets serve as wonderful wall hooks suitable for any number of purposes.

Above ~ Ornate, embellished details like this opulent chandelier give even the tightest spot a sense of grandeur.

Opposite ~ Case in point—a chandelier really makes this dining room/wine cellar (in the basement of a 1930s bungalow) look like you are supping in a French château. Grape-gathering crates were stacked to create the wine racks, and an old oak farm table is surrounded by mismatched French-style chairs.

Opposite ~ WHEN IN DOUBT whether your "high" is high enough, throw in a crystal chandelier.

Above ~ THIS BATHROOM shows that you don't need a lot of space to get just the right mix of high and low. The opposition of the frames (high/low, big/small) and the clever staggered mounting make for incredible visual interest.

CHAPTER NINE

"BOY" MEETS "GIRL"

WHY DO OPPOSITES ATTRACT? Perhaps we're just wired that way. There's something electric. A spark is ignited, and the rest is history.

Some people have a preference for harder edges and heft, while others can't get enough of the romance evoked by flowers and ruffles. A house does not get much more romantic than the Beekman farmhouse. With its wrap-around porch and elaborate balustrade, you can easily see why the *New York Times* called it a "wedding cake house."

With our love for modern and industrial design, it was easy for us to "play against type"—and, like all good love affairs, we think the house and its furnishings are inseparable.

Stereotypes aside, there are no greater forces in nature than the masculine and the feminine. They both exist in each of us. In Chinese philosophy, yin and yang describe how apparently opposite or contrary forces are actually complementary, interconnected, and interdependent in the natural world and give rise to each other as they interrelate. They are forces that interact to form a dynamic system in which the whole is greater than the assembled parts.

And this is exactly what a home should be.

Opposite ~ The Beekman house exterior.

All ions are charged, which means that like all charged objects they are attracted to opposite electric charges and repelled by like charges.
—*THE TEXTBOOK OF ELEMENTAL CHEMISTRY*

Though this kitchen has plenty of frills, the design is successful because of the wise choice of color, Benjamin Moore's Iced Slate. The rush-seat stools were originally mahogany brown and an eyesore, but that was nothing a little elbow grease and white paint couldn't tackle.

Opposite ~ IN THIS MASTER BEDROOM, a traditional four-poster walnut bed stands in striking juxtaposition with the exuberant kilim-covered ottoman. Don't be afraid to mix colors and patterns that most people wouldn't. The more action in the room, the more memorable.

Above ~ WE LOVE ROOMS that make us ask, "Who lives here?" This sitting area in a guest room does just that with a collection of antiques and vintage finds. The Victorian dress form adds a little whimsy, and every room you live in should have a bit of that.

Opposite ~ RELIVE YOUR FIRST SCHOOL-AGE CRUSH in a room with bits of nostalgia. The lesson for the day here is one in asymmetry. Create visual interest in a room by hanging wall art off-of-center or displaying objects (like the books and trophy on the floor) in unexpected places.

Above ~ WITH ITS WROUGHT-IRON CANOPY BED and the dreamy linens, this bedroom was balanced by painting the walls dark and adding some hunting paraphernalia.

IMAGINE THIS ROOM with a more ornate coffee table and a side table or table lamp. The whole energy of the room would change. The patterned pillows and the fringed throws need a little heavy metal to make the room really sing.

These dark bentwood chairs and rustic oak table are perfectly fine, but it's the addition of the linen table runners that makes this setting ethereal.

WITH ITS MIX of toile and polka dots, this bedroom could have been a nightmare, but the simple lines of the bed help keep everything in check.

IN THIS ROOM, you see how two different decorating styles
can come together. A little floral and a little industrial are
tied together by a neutral palette.

IF YOU LOVE LAYERS of dreamy romantic patterns, make a more effective statement by grounding them a little with a massive piece of furniture like this bed.

Looking in magazines or through design blogs, you might be led to think that you must have an antiques or thrift store next door to create a room with character, but that's just not true. You only need a good eye. In this bedroom, the wallpaper with a large-scale motif from Anthropologie eliminates the need for art. The bed is from Pier 1, the gingham duvet from West Elm, and the nightstands from the backyard—really!

THE HEAVY HEADBOARD makes a pattern-rich wallpaper
less overwhelming in this bedroom.

THIS LIVING ROOM's built-in shelves show off a collection of vintage boxes in hues—honey, green, red—that echo the floral upholstery. It's a brilliant use of this collection. The very linear arrangement manages to make this room feel modern even though nothing in the room actually is.

Here a very masculine bed gives a respite from the field
of floral patterns in which it sits.

Above ~ A SETTEE AND TWO ARMCHAIRS from Restoration
Hardware cozy up to a Zentique coffee table. The boat pro-
peller adds interest to this living room in an 18th-century
Connecticut home.

Above ~ QUICK FIXES can make a world of difference. In this bedroom, a linen tablecloth was draped over an upholstered headboard, adding softness to the room and a subtle sense of depth. The different presentation styles of the paintings above the bed show that two distinct personalities share this space.

Following spread ~ WHEN BOY MEETS GIRL and they move in together, perfect harmony can be achieved (with a little forethought). In this bedroom, a '50s-era settee sidles up to an iron bed by Pottery Barn. A pine chest and a round table take the place of matchy-matchy nightstands.

THIS ROOM CAPTURES the romance of camping (without
actually having to rough it). Notice the use of vintage
board games as art on the shelves.

PEOPLE WHO LOVE ANTIQUES sometimes don't know when to stop, and they crowd a room with all the things they love. This can do a real disservice to the beauty of the pieces. Here the flourishes of Victorian furniture are better displayed with minimalist restraint.

Above ~ THERE ARE VERY FEW MEN who would acquiesce to a room painted pink, but the furnishings here make the color an afterthought.

Opposite ~ THE GRAPHIC PILLOWS and a few pops of yellow are all that it took to turn what could have been a man-cave fishing camp into a love nest.

Opposite ~ Many young couples or new home owners don't have a lot of spare coin to put into décor. Just tell all your friends that you have a "minimalist style" and use some of the tips found in this book to create a livable, lovable space that stands out. This room is a mattress on the floor, has no window treatments, and features minimal décor, but the personality of the couple shines through.

Above ~ The "in-between" colors of this room allow the mood of the room to change with the light of day, creating the perfect atmosphere whenever your gentleman comes calling.

Following spread ~ In this small room, dark charcoal brown was used on the walls to create the illusion of depth. The floors were painted a lighter shade of gray. Contrasting color and texture come from the pink pillows and weathered woods.

HOUSE MEETS HOME

Did the world need another book about decorating your home? We would argue "yes," but we don't have to. Others have stated over and over its importance:

"HOME IS NOT WHERE YOU HAVE TO GO but where you want to go; nor is it a place where you are sullenly admitted, but rather where you are welcomed—by the people, the walls, the tiles on the floor, the flowers beside the door, the play of light, the very grass."
—SCOTT RUSSELL SANDERS

"A HOME FILLED WITH NOTHING BUT YOURSELF. It's heavy, that lightness. It's crushing, that emptiness."
—MARGARET ATWOOD, THE TENT

"THE ORNAMENT OF A HOUSE is the friends who frequent it."
—RALPH WALDO EMERSON

"A HOUSE from which nobody ever went away without feeling better in some way . . . a house in which there was always laughter. . . ."
—L.M. MONTGOMERY

"ONLY WHERE THERE IS LIFE can there be home."
—JOYCE CAROL OATES

"DEAR LITTLE HOUSE THAT I HAVE LIVED IN, there is happiness you have seen, even before I was born. In you is my life, and all the people I have loved are a part of you, so to go out of you, and leave you, is to leave myself."
—RICHARD LLEWELLYN, HOW GREEN WAS MY VALLEY

"I DON'T MEAN what other people mean when they speak of a home, because I don't regard a home as a . . . well, as a place, a building . . . a house . . . of wood, bricks, stone. I think of a home as being a thing that two people have between them in which each can . . . well, nest."
—TENNESSEE WILLIAMS

"OUR HOME tells a story about us, so we may as well take the opportunity to make it a stylish one."
—DEBORAH NEEDLEMAN, THE PERFECTLY IMPERFECT HOME

"DESPITE THE OPPOSITION AND TENSIONS THAT ATTRACT AND BIND US, we are really all made up of the same desires and the same matter."
—BRENT RIDGE + JOSH KILMER-PURCELL, BEEKMAN 1802

PHOTO CREDITS

INDEX

Boldface page references indicate photographs.

THERE IS NO DIFFERENCE BETWEEN TIME AND ANY
OF THE THREE DIMENSIONS OF SPACE. . . .
WHAT GOES UP MUST COME DOWN. . . . ANY TWO BODIES IN
THE UNIVERSE ATTRACT EACH OTHER WITH A FORCE
THAT IS DIRECTLY PROPORTIONAL TO THE PRODUCT OF
THEIR MASSES. . . . THE EARLIEST CHINESE MAGNETIC
COMPASSES WERE PROBABLY NOT DESIGNED FOR
NAVIGATION BUT RATHER TO ORDER AND HARMONIZE THEIR
ENVIRONMENTS. . . . THE WHOLE IS GREATER THAN THE
SUM OF ITS PARTS. . . . FOR EVERY ACTION, THERE IS AN
EQUAL AND OPPOSITE REACTION. . . . TROPISM: THE
TURNING OF ALL OR PART OF AN ORGANISM IN A
PARTICULAR DIRECTION IN RESPONSE TO AN EXTERNAL
STIMULUS. . . . ALL CHARGED OBJECTS ARE ATTRACTED TO
OPPOSITE ELECTRIC CHARGES. . . . NEWTON DECLARED
THAT COLORS OPPOSITE EACH OTHER HAD THE
STRONGEST CONTRAST AND HARMONY. . . .